Confessing the Hebrew Scriptures

Adonai Yireh –

יְהֹוָה יִרְאֶה

"THE LORD WILL PROVIDE"

Published by Jewish Voice Ministries International
PO Box 31998
Phoenix, AZ 85046-1998

Printed in China

ISBN 978-0-9821117-7-2

Confessing the Hebrew Scriptures

Adonai Yireh –

יְהוָ֥ה יִרְאֶ֑ה

"THE LORD WILL PROVIDE"

Jonathan Bernis

INTRODUCTION FROM JONATHAN BERNIS

The Power of Confession

It is my hope and prayer that this workbook, Volume 3 in my **Confessing the Hebrew Scriptures** series, will prove to be a rich blessing to your life. Over my 30+ years in ministry I have seen the fruit of confession of the Word of God. Through the process of confessing and hearing the Word, I have seen many healed, delivered and transformed. Proverbs 18:21 declares, *"death and life are in the power of the tongue."* Our confession can bring either blessings or curses upon us and those we love. It is God's desire that we use our tongues to produce blessing, life, and faith according to His Word. So how do we accomplish this? How do we incorporate this biblical truth to work in our lives? The biblical principle is so very simple:

> *"So then faith cometh by hearing, and hearing by the word of God."* —Romans 10:17, KJV

From this verse, we understand that faith is built in us as we hear the Word of God. Notice, though, that hearing is mentioned twice. I believe this is because there are two kinds of hearing: hearing with our natural ears and hearing with the ears of our spirit. This is the process by which faith is deposited and released in our lives. We hear the Word of God as it is read and confessed, and over time, as we hear God's promises over and over again, it eventually drops down into our spirit, where our faith is then activated. When this incredible process happens, the promises of God become a reality in our life. This simple truth is what brings us into the reality of the salvation experience:

> *"For with the heart man believeth unto righteousness;*
> *and with the mouth confession is made unto salvation."* —Romans 10:1,0 KJV

This is what **biblical** confession is all about. It's about getting HIS Word… (which incidentally is His will) into our hearts, into our spirits. That's where faith must dwell in order to be activated—not the mind. Not only do we experience God's provision of salvation in this manner, but also all of the other promises given to us in Scripture are based on the same principle of "believing with the heart and confessing unto." *The blessings God has provided for us in His Word, such as healing and health, deliverance, divine provision, and supernatural peace and comfort are all realized in exactly the same way. Every promise and blessing of God is acquired through faith. But without faith, it is impossible to please Him* (Hebrews 11:6).

When God called Joshua to lead the Children of Israel into the Promised Land after the death of Moses, He gave him the following instructions:

> *Only be strong and very courageous, that you may observe to do*
> *according to all the law which Moses My servant commanded you;*
> *do not turn from it to the right hand or to the left, that you may*

prosper wherever you go. This Book of the Law shall not depart from your mouth, but you shall meditate in it day and night, that you may observe to do according to all that is written in it. For then you will make your way prosperous, and then you will have good success. —Joshua 1:7-8

While the Christian concept of meditation is derived from the Latin word "to consider or contemplate" and has more to do with reflection—the process of deliberately focusing on specific Scriptures and reflecting on their meaning—the Hebrew has two concepts or a "dual concept" of meditation. The first, (*seecha*) has to do with rehearing in one's mind or thoughts and is similar to the Christian concept of meditation. The other, (*hagah*) is not reflection with the *mind*, but with the *mouth*—to rehearse the Word of God in speech, "to speak, talk, utter, or mutter." This is the Hebrew word used in the above text. It is this concept and practice of meditation that the Lord tells Joshua will make him both *"prosperous and successful."*

It stands to reason that if God told Joshua that confession of His Word would make him prosperous and successful, then we also can experience the same prosperity and success he experienced if we follow the same principles.

The Significance of Hebrew

While most of us understand that the Old Testament Scriptures were written primarily in the Hebrew language, very few of us can actually read or understand Hebrew. Therefore, we are forced to read the various English translations of the Bible. And while there are many excellent translations out there, they often miss the nuances, insight, and deeper revelation found in the original Hebrew.

For example, God reveals Himself through different Hebrew names in the Tanakh (Old Testament). Names such as El Shaddai God Almighty, Adonai-Tzidkaynu The LORD our Righteousness, Adonai-Nissi The LORD our Banner, Adonai-Rofecha The LORD our Healer and Adonai-Shalom The LORD our Peace (see my previous workbooks on these), and now Adonai-Yireh The LORD will Provide. These names reveal His character, His attributes, His very nature. When we dig into these names in the Hebrew, we gain extraordinary insight into who the LORD is and what He has provided for us. The benefits promised to us in the Bible, promises of healing and health, salvation, deliverance, divine provision, supernatural peace, and so on are all originally in Hebrew.

So, while there is no doubt that because the LORD is omniscient, He responds to any language and that confession of the Word of God in any language is going to release power and blessing. If we want to experience the greatest impact, the greatest depth, and the fullest meaning, we must go back to the roots. And those roots are Hebrew. The ancient Hebrew sages taught that although it was permissible to pray in other languages, praying in **Lashon HaKodesh**, the Holy Tongue, was always preferable, even if the person did not understand the words.

How to Use the Workbook and CD

You may be saying to yourself at this point, "This is all well and good, but how can I do this?" How is this possible—to confess the Scriptures in the original Hebrew without going to Bible school or seminary, without undertaking an extensive study of Hebrew? The good news is there is a way. The answer is found in a system developed by the Reform Movement of American Judaism.

As Jews immigrated to America in the late 19th and early part of the 20th century from the "Old Country" of Eastern and Central Europe to forge a new life free from the bitter anti-Semitism they had endured for so long, they quickly began to assimilate into American culture. Hebrew education, which was a mandatory part of their former prayer life (as well as Yiddish as a spoken language) began to disappear. In order to preserve Hebrew prayer in their synagogues, a method called transliteration was employed. This simple process, which we see utilized in dictionaries, uses English letters to sound out the Hebrew words. In other words, the Hebrew text is converted to English in order to read and pronounce the original Hebrew.

Let's look at a few examples to understand how this works:

- The Hebrew word for "peace" is *Shalom* שָׁלוֹם

  While you may recognize this Hebrew word from seeing it often enough, most cannot read the actual Hebrew characters. But when we use the transliteration method, it now becomes very readable: **sha•lome**

- Let's try another one. The Hebrew word for Jerusalem is יְרוּשָׁלַיִם

  While few can read the actual Hebrew, when we apply the transliteration method, it becomes easy: **Ye•roo•sha•la•yim**

And off you go. It's that easy. No seminary training, no intensive Hebrew study. Just begin to work through the pages using this simple yet effective transliteration method, and you will be confessing the Scriptures in the ancient Hebrew tongue!

The Origin of "Adonai Yireh" (The Lord Will Provide)

In Genesis 22, God tested Abraham by asking him to sacrifice his only son Isaac. Abraham obeys and takes him to a place called Moriah, which today is the current site of the temple mount in Jerusalem. When Isaac, (who is likely a teenager by this time) sees that the wood and fire are prepared but there is no offering, he starts to realize what is happening. He nervously asks his father "where is the lamb for the burnt offering? Abraham, filled with faith, responds "God himself will provide the lamb". In Hebrew, יִרְאֶה אֱלֹהִים (Elohim Yireh) literally "*God will provide.*" Not only does Abraham believe that God will provide an alternative sacrifice to save his son Isaac, he is also prophesying the sacrifice of God's only son Yeshua on the same location, an event that would take place almost 2,000 years later!

After seeing Abrahams obedience and faith, God does, indeed, spare Isaac and provide a lamb for the sacrifice. We are told in verse 14 that Abraham then names the place " יְהוָה ׀ יִרְאֶה (Adonai Yireh) *the Lord will provide* or *the Lord will be seen or see to it*" because the Lord saw his need and responded.

I have chosen to use the title from verse 14, "the **Lord** who provides."

Each page has a Scripture promise relating to יִרְאֶה (the word used by the Jewish community in substitution for the Hebrew name translated LORD, the Tetragrammaton, often pronounced Jehovah or Yaweh) Yireh: The Lord Will Provide and contains the text in Hebrew, English, and English Transliteration directly from the Hebrew.

Along with the workbook, we've included a companion CD so you can hear how each Scripture sounds when spoken by a native Israeli Hebrew speaker. I suggest you begin by playing the CD and following along in the English and transliterated Hebrew from Scripture to Scripture. The numbers in the lower left corner of each page correspond to the track number on your audio CD. After, try confessing the Hebrew transliteration along with the CD to learn which syllables to accent. In no time, you will be confessing these Scriptures in Hebrew just like a native-born Israeli. It really is that easy!

Finally, let me share with you four things to keep in mind as you put these Hebrew prayers to work for God to bring peace into your life:

1. **Let the Scriptures fill your heart.** As you pray and confess these powerful promises of God, ask Him to make the Word come alive in your life. Watch as your faith grows on a daily basis!

2. **Be confident in the goodness of God.** Since these prayers are taken directly from the Hebrew Scriptures, you can know that you are praying perfectly in line with God's will for your life.

3. **Confession is a simple act of trust and obedience.** This is not some mysterious, mystical act. It is simply believing and acting on the truth of God's Word. As you are diligent to exercise this powerful principle in your life day by day, you will be amazed as you watch it take hold in your life and result in transformation.

4. **Know that God's promises are true.** I encourage you to confess these promises of healing and health boldly and with expectation that you and your loved ones will experience exactly what God promises He will do. Remember, God is the same yesterday, today, and forever.

You may wish to read through the entire book at one sitting. You may choose to take one prayer in order each day during your personal time with God. You may find specific Scriptures are particularly meaningful in your specific situation and want to listen to them again and again. No matter how you utilize this workbook, I have no doubt that if you exercise this powerful principle of confessing God's Word in your daily devotions, it **will** bear fruit. You **will** be changed…

"So shall My word be that goes forth from My mouth; It shall not return to Me void,
But it shall accomplish what I please, And it shall prosper in the thing for which I sent it." —Isaiah 55:11

Jonathan Bernis, Phoenix, Arizona

CONFESSING THE HEBREW SCRIPTURES

Adonai Yireh – יְהֹוָה יִרְאֶה
"THE LORD WILL PROVIDE"

*T*hen Abraham lifted up his eyes and behold, there was a ram, just caught in the thick bushes by its horns. So Abraham went and took the ram, and offered it up as a burnt offering instead of his son. Abraham named that place, ADONAI Yireh,—as it is said today, "On the mountain, ADONAI will provide.

Genesis 22:13,14

וַיִּשָּׂא אַבְרָהָם אֶת-עֵינָיו וַיַּרְא וְהִנֵּה-אַיִל אַחַר נֶאֱחַז בַּסְּבַךְ
בְּקַרְנָיו וַיֵּלֶךְ אַבְרָהָם וַיִּקַּח אֶת-הָאַיִל וַיַּעֲלֵהוּ לְעֹלָה תַּחַת בְּנוֹ.
וַיִּקְרָא אַבְרָהָם שֵׁם-הַמָּקוֹם הַהוּא יְהֹוָה יִרְאֶה אֲשֶׁר יֵאָמֵר
הַיּוֹם בְּהַר יְהֹוָה יֵרָאֶה.

Va•yi•sa Av•ra•hám et - ei•nav va•yar ve•hi•né - á•yil a•char
ne•e•chaz bas•vach be•kar•nav va•yé•lech Av•ra•hám
va•yi•kách et - ha•á•yil va•ya•alé•hu le•ola tá•chat b'no.
Va•yik•ra Av•ra•hám shem - ha•ma•kom ha•hú Adonái
Yir•éh ashér ye•a•mer ha•yom be•Har Adonái ye•ra•éh.

Track 01

CONFESSING THE HEBREW SCRIPTURES

Adonai Yireh – יְהֹוָה יִרְאֶה
"THE LORD WILL PROVIDE"

May God give you—from the dew of the sky and from the fatness of the land—an abundance of grain and new wine.

Genesis 27:28

וְיִתֶּן־לְךָ הָאֱלֹהִים מִטַּל הַשָּׁמַיִם וּמִשְׁמַנֵּי הָאָרֶץ וְרֹב דָּגָן וְתִירֹשׁ.

Ve•yi•ten - le•chá ha•Elohím mi•tal ha•sha•má•yim
oo•mish•ma•néi ha•á•retz ve•rov da•gan ve•ti•rosh.

Track 02

CONFESSING THE HEBREW SCRIPTURES

Adonai Yireh – יְהוָה יִרְאֶה
"THE LORD WILL PROVIDE"

If you walk in My statutes, keep My mitzvot and carry them out then I will give you rains in their season, the land will yield its crops, and the trees of the field will yield their fruit.

Leviticus 26:3,4

אִם-בְּחֻקֹּתַי תֵּלֵכוּ וְאֶת-מִצְוֹתַי תִּשְׁמְרוּ וַעֲשִׂיתֶם אֹתָם. וְנָתַתִּי גִשְׁמֵיכֶם בְּעִתָּם וְנָתְנָה הָאָרֶץ יְבוּלָהּ וְעֵץ הַשָּׂדֶה יִתֵּן פִּרְיוֹ.

Eem - be•chu•ko•tái te•lé•chu ve•et - mitz•vo•tái tish•me•ru
va•asi•tem o•tam. Ve•na•ta•tí gish•mei•chem be•ee•tam
ve•nat•na ha•á•retz ye•vu•láh ve•etz ha•sa•dé yi•ten pir•yo.

CONFESSING THE HEBREW SCRIPTURES

Adonai Yireh – יְהֹוָה יִרְאֶה
"THE LORD WILL PROVIDE"

ADONAI your God, who goes before you, He Himself will fight for you— just as He did for you in Egypt before your own eyes, and in the wilderness, where you saw how ADONAI your God carried you as a man carries his son, everywhere you went until you came to this place.'

Deuteronomy 1:30,31

יְהֹוָה אֱלֹהֵיכֶם הַהֹלֵךְ לִפְנֵיכֶם הוּא יִלָּחֵם לָכֶם כְּכֹל אֲשֶׁר עָשָׂה אִתְּכֶם בְּמִצְרַיִם לְעֵינֵיכֶם. וּבַמִּדְבָּר אֲשֶׁר רָאִיתָ אֲשֶׁר נְשָׂאֲךָ יְהֹוָה אֱלֹהֶיךָ כַּאֲשֶׁר יִשָּׂא־אִישׁ אֶת־בְּנוֹ בְּכָל־הַדֶּרֶךְ אֲשֶׁר הֲלַכְתֶּם עַד־בֹּאֲכֶם עַד־הַמָּקוֹם הַזֶּה.

Adonái Elo•hey•chem ha•ho•lech lif•nei•chem hoo
yi•la•chém la•chém ke•chol ashér asa eet•chem
be•Mitz•rá•yim le•ei•ne•chem. Oo•va•mid•bar ashér
ra•ée•ta ashér ne•sa•a•chá Adonái Elo•hé•cha ka•a•shér
yi•sa - eesh et - b'no be•chol - ha•dé•rech ashér ha•lach•tem
ad bo•a•chem ad - ha•ma•kom ha•zé.

Track 04

CONFESSING THE HEBREW SCRIPTURES

Adonai Yireh – יְהֹוָה יִרְאֶה
"THE LORD WILL PROVIDE"

He will love you, bless you and multiply you. He will also bless the fruit of your womb and the produce of your soil, your grain and your new wine and your oil, the increase of your herds and the young of your flock, in the land that He swore to your fathers to give you.

Deuteronomy 7:13

וְאֵהֵבְךָ וּבֵרַכְךָ וְהִרְבֶּךָ וּבֵרַךְ פְּרִי-בִטְנְךָ וּפְרִי-אַדְמָתְךָ דְּגָנְךָ
וְתִירֹשְׁךָ וְיִצְהָרֶךָ שְׁגַר-אֲלָפֶיךָ וְעַשְׁתְּרֹת צֹאנֶךָ עַל הָאֲדָמָה
אֲשֶׁר-נִשְׁבַּע לַאֲבֹתֶיךָ לָתֶת לָךְ.

Va•a•hev•cha oo•ve•ra•che•cha ve•hir•bé•cha
oo•ve•rach pe•ri - vit•ne•cha oof•ri - ad•ma•té•cha
de•gan•cha ve•ti•rosh•cha ve•yitz•ha•ré•cha
sh'gar - ala•fé•cha ve•ash•te•rot tzo•né•cha al
ha•ada•ma ashér - nish•ba la•avo•té•cha lá•tet lach.

CONFESSING THE HEBREW SCRIPTURES

Adonai Yireh – יְהֹוָה יִרְאֶה
"THE LORD WILL PROVIDE"

For ADONAI your God is bringing you into a good land—a land of wadis with water, of springs and fountains flowing out in the valleys and hills, a land of wheat and barley, vines, figs and pomegranates, a land of olive oil and honey, a land where you will eat bread with no poverty, where you will lack nothing, a land whose stones are iron, and out of whose hills you can dig copper.

Deuteronomy 8:7-9

כִּי יְהֹוָה אֱלֹהֶיךָ מְבִיאֲךָ אֶל-אֶרֶץ טוֹבָה אֶרֶץ נַחֲלֵי מָיִם עֲיָנֹת
וּתְהֹמֹת יֹצְאִים בַּבִּקְעָה וּבָהָר. אֶרֶץ חִטָּה וּשְׂעֹרָה וְגֶפֶן וּתְאֵנָה
וְרִמּוֹן אֶרֶץ-זֵית שֶׁמֶן וּדְבָשׁ. אֶרֶץ אֲשֶׁר לֹא בְמִסְכֵּנֻת תֹּאכַל-בָּהּ
לֶחֶם לֹא-תֶחְסַר כֹּל בָּהּ אֶרֶץ אֲשֶׁר אֲבָנֶיהָ בַרְזֶל וּמֵהֲרָרֶיהָ
תַּחְצֹב נְחֹשֶׁת.

Ki Adonái Elo·hé·cha mevi·a·cha el - é·retz to·va é·retz
ná·cha·lei má·yim aya·not oo·te·ho·mot yotz·eem
ba·bik·ah oo·va·har. Éretz chi·ta oo·se·ora ve·gé·fen
oo·te·ena ve·rimon é·retz - zeit shé·men ood·vásh.
Éretz ashér lo ve·mis·ke·noot to·chal - báh lé·chem
lo - tech·sar kol báh é·retz ashér ava·né·ha var·zel
oo·me·ha·ra·ré·ha tach·tzov ne·chó·shet.

CONFESSING THE HEBREW SCRIPTURES

Adonai Yireh – יְהֹוָה יִרְאֶה
"THE LORD WILL PROVIDE"

ADONAI will command the blessing on you in your barns and in every undertaking of your hand, and He will bless you in the land ADONAI your God is giving you.

Deuteronomy 28:8

יְצַו יְהֹוָה אִתְּךָ אֶת-הַבְּרָכָה בַּאֲסָמֶיךָ וּבְכֹל מִשְׁלַח יָדֶךָ וּבֵרַכְךָ
בָּאָרֶץ אֲשֶׁר-יְהֹוָה אֱלֹהֶיךָ נֹתֵן לָךְ׃

Ye•tzav Adonái eet•cha et - ha•be•ra•cha ba•asa•mé•cha oo•ve•chol mish•lach
ya•dé•cha oo•vera•che•cha ba•á•retz ashér - Adonái Elo•hé•cha no•ten lach.

Confessing the Hebrew Scriptures

Adonai Yireh – יְהֹוָה יִרְאֶה
"THE LORD WILL PROVIDE"

So keep the words of this covenant and do them, so that you may prosper in all that you do.

Deuteronomy 29:8

וּשְׁמַרְתֶּם אֶת־דִּבְרֵי הַבְּרִית הַזֹּאת וַעֲשִׂיתֶם אֹתָם לְמַעַן
תַּשְׂכִּילוּ אֵת כָּל־אֲשֶׁר תַּעֲשׂוּן.

Oosh•mar•tem et - div•réi ha•be•rit ha•zot va•asi•tem
o•tam le•má•an tas•kí•lu et kol - ashér ta•a•soon.

Track 08

CONFESSING THE HEBREW SCRIPTURES

Adonai Yireh – יְהוָֹה יִרְאֶה

"THE LORD WILL PROVIDE"

This book of the Torah should not depart from your mouth—you are to meditate on it day and night, so that you may be careful to do everything written in it. For then you will make your ways prosperous and then you will be successful.

Joshua 1:8

לֹא-יָמוּשׁ סֵפֶר הַתּוֹרָה הַזֶּה מִפִּיךָ וְהָגִיתָ בּוֹ יוֹמָם וָלַיְלָה לְמַעַן תִּשְׁמֹר לַעֲשׂוֹת כְּכָל-הַכָּתוּב בּוֹ כִּי-אָז תַּצְלִיחַ אֶת-דְּרָכֶךָ וְאָז תַּשְׂכִּיל.

Lo - ya•moosh Sé•fer ha•Toráh ha•zé mi•pí•cha
ve•ha•gí•ta bo yo•mam va•lái•la le•má•an tish•mor
la•a•sot ke•chol - ha•ka•toov bo ki - az tatz•lí•ach
et - de•ra•ché•cha ve•az tas•kil.

Confessing the Hebrew Scriptures

Adonai Yireh – יְהֹוָה יִרְאֶה
"THE LORD WILL PROVIDE"

ADONAI makes poor and makes rich, He brings low and also lifts up. He raises the helpless from the dust. He lifts the needy from the dunghill, to make them sit with nobles, granting them a seat of honor. For the earth's pillars are ADONAI's, and He has set the world on them.

I Samuel 2:7,8

יְהֹוָה מוֹרִישׁ וּמַעֲשִׁיר מַשְׁפִּיל אַף-מְרוֹמֵם. מֵקִים מֵעָפָר דָּל
מֵאַשְׁפֹּת יָרִים אֶבְיוֹן לְהוֹשִׁיב עִם-נְדִיבִים וְכִסֵּא כָבוֹד יַנְחִלֵם כִּי
לַיהֹוָה מְצֻקֵי אֶרֶץ וַיָּשֶׁת עֲלֵיהֶם תֵּבֵל.

Adonái mo•rish oo•ma•a•shir mash•pil af - me•ro•mem.
Me•kim me•a•far dal me•ash•pot ya•rim ev•yon le•ho•shiv
eem - ne•di•vim ve•chi•sé cha•vod yan•chi•lem ki la•Adonái
me•tzu•kéi é•retz va•yá•shet a•lei•hém te•vél.

Confessing the Hebrew Scriptures

Adonai Yireh – יְהֹוָה יִרְאֶה
"THE LORD WILL PROVIDE"

Keep the charge of ADONAI your God, to walk in His ways, to keep His statutes, His commandments, His ordinances, and His decrees, according to what is written in the Torah of Moses, so that you may succeed in all that you do and wherever you turn

1 Kings 2:3

וְשָׁמַרְתָּ אֶת-מִשְׁמֶרֶת יְהוָה אֱלֹהֶיךָ לָלֶכֶת בִּדְרָכָיו לִשְׁמֹר חֻקֹּתָיו
מִצְוֺתָיו וּמִשְׁפָּטָיו וְעֵדְוֺתָיו כַּכָּתוּב בְּתוֹרַת מֹשֶׁה לְמַעַן תַּשְׂכִּיל
אֵת כָּל-אֲשֶׁר תַּעֲשֶׂה וְאֵת כָּל-אֲשֶׁר תִּפְנֶה שָׁם.

Ve•sha•mar•tá et - mish•mé•ret Adonái Elo•hé•cha la•lé•chet
bid•ra•chav lish•mor chu•ko•tav mitz•vo•tav oo•mish•pa•tav
ve•edvo•tav ka•ka•toov be•Torát Mo•shé le•má•an tas•kil
et kol - ashér ta•asé ve•et kol - ashér tif•né sham.

CONFESSING THE HEBREW SCRIPTURES

Adonai Yireh – יְהֹוָה יִרְאֶה
"THE LORD WILL PROVIDE"

Both riches and honor come from You. You rule over everything. In Your hand is power and might, in Your hand, to magnify and give strength to all.

1 Chronicles 29:12

וְהָעֹשֶׁר וְהַכָּבוֹד מִלְּפָנֶיךָ וְאַתָּה מוֹשֵׁל בַּכֹּל וּבְיָדְךָ כֹּחַ וּגְבוּרָה
וּבְיָדְךָ לְגַדֵּל וּלְחַזֵּק לַכֹּל.

Ve·ha·ó·sher ve·ha·ka·vod mil·fa·né·cha ve·ata mo·shel
ba·kol oo·ve·yad·cha kó·ach oog·vu·ra oo·ve·yad·cha
le·ga·del oo·le·cha·zék la·kol.

CONFESSING THE HEBREW SCRIPTURES

Adonai Yireh – יְהוָֹה יִרְאֶה

"THE LORD WILL PROVIDE"

He continued to seek God in the days of Zechariah, who had understanding through the visions of God. As long as he sought ADONAI, God made him prosper.

2 Chronicles 26:5

וַיְהִי לִדְרֹשׁ אֱלֹהִים בִּימֵי זְכַרְיָהוּ הַמֵּבִין בִּרְאוֹת הָאֱלֹהִים וּבִימֵי דָרְשׁוֹ אֶת־יְהוָֹה הִצְלִיחוֹ הָאֱלֹהִים.

Va•ye•hi lid•rosh Elohím biy•mey Ze•char•yáhoo ha•me•vin bir•ot ha•Elohím oo•vi•méi dor•sho et - Adonái hitz•li•chó ha•Elohím.

CONFESSING THE HEBREW SCRIPTURES

Adonai Yireh – יְהֹוָה יִרְאֶה
"THE LORD WILL PROVIDE"

For forty years You sustained them in the desert: they lacked nothing, their garments did not wear out and their feet did not swell.

Nehemiah 9:21

וְאַרְבָּעִים שָׁנָה כִּלְכַּלְתָּם בַּמִּדְבָּר לֹא חָסֵרוּ שַׂלְמֹתֵיהֶם לֹא בָלוּ וְרַגְלֵיהֶם לֹא בָצֵקוּ.

Ve·ar·ba·eem sha·na kil·kal·tam ba·mid·bar lo cha·sé·ru sal·mo·tei·hém lo va·lu ve·rag·lei·hém lo va·tzé·ku.

Track 14

Confessing the Hebrew Scriptures

Adonai Yireh – יְרָאֶה יְהֹוָה

"THE LORD WILL PROVIDE"

Happy is the one who has not walked in the advice of the wicked, nor stood in the way of sinners, nor sat in the seat of scoffers. But his delight is in the Torah of ADONAI, and on His Torah he meditates day and night. He will be like a planted tree over streams of water, producing its fruit during its season. Its leaf never droops— but in all he does, he succeeds.

Psalms 1:1-3

אַשְׁרֵי הָאִישׁ אֲשֶׁר לֹא הָלַךְ בַּעֲצַת רְשָׁעִים וּבְדֶרֶךְ חַטָּאִים לֹא
עָמָד וּבְמוֹשַׁב לֵצִים לֹא יָשָׁב. כִּי אִם-בְּתוֹרַת יְהֹוָה חֶפְצוֹ וּבְתוֹרָתוֹ
יֶהְגֶּה יוֹמָם וָלָיְלָה. וְהָיָה כְּעֵץ שָׁתוּל עַל-פַּלְגֵי מָיִם אֲשֶׁר פִּרְיוֹ יִתֵּן
בְּעִתּוֹ וְעָלֵהוּ לֹא יִבּוֹל וְכֹל אֲשֶׁר-יַעֲשֶׂה יַצְלִיחַ.

Ash•réi ha•eesh ashér lo ha•lach ba•a•tzat re•sha•eem
oo•ve•dé•rech cha•ta•eem lo amad oo•ve•mo•shav le•tzim
lo ya•shav. Ki eem - be•Torát Adonái chef•tzo oo•ve•Tora•to
ye•he•gé yo•mam va•lái•la. Ve•ha•ya ke•etz sha•tool
al - pal•géi má•yim ashér pir•yo yi•ten be•ee•to ve•a•lé•hu
lo yi•bol ve•chol ashér - ya•a•sé yatz•lí•ach.

Track 15

CONFESSING THE HEBREW SCRIPTURES

Adonai Yireh – יְהֹוָה יִרְאֶה
"THE LORD WILL PROVIDE"

But You, ADONAI, are a shield around me, my glory and the lifter of my head. I cry out to ADONAI with my voice, and He answers me from His holy mountain. Selah I lie down and sleep. I awake—for ADONAI sustains me.

Psalms 3:4-6

וְאַתָּה יְהוָה מָגֵן בַּעֲדִי כְּבוֹדִי וּמֵרִים רֹאשִׁי. קוֹלִי אֶל-יְהוָה אֶקְרָא וַיַּעֲנֵנִי מֵהַר קָדְשׁוֹ סֶלָה. אֲנִי שָׁכַבְתִּי וָאִישָׁנָה הֱקִיצוֹתִי כִּי יְהוָה יִסְמְכֵנִי.

Ve•ata Adonái ma•gen ba•adi ke•vo•di oo•me•rim ro•shi.
Ko•li el - Adonái ek•ra va•ya•a•né•ni me•har kod•sho Séla.
Ani sha•cháv•ti va•ee•shá•na heki•tzó•ti ki Adonái
yis•me•ché•ni.

CONFESSING THE HEBREW SCRIPTURES

Adonai Yireh – יְהֹוָה יִרְאֶה
"THE LORD WILL PROVIDE"

May He grant you your heart's desire and fulfill all your plans. We will shout for joy in your victory and lift up our banners in the Name of our God! May ADONAI fulfill all your petitions.

Psalms 20:5,6

יִתֶּן-לְךָ כִלְבָבֶךָ וְכָל-עֲצָתְךָ יְמַלֵּא. נְרַנְּנָה בִּישׁוּעָתֶךָ וּבְשֵׁם-אֱלֹהֵינוּ
נִדְגֹּל יְמַלֵּא יְהֹוָה כָּל-מִשְׁאֲלוֹתֶיךָ.

Yi•ten - le•chá chil•va•vé•cha ve•chol - atzat•cha ye•ma•lé.
N'ra•ne•na bi•ye•shu•a•té•cha oo•ve•shem - Elo•héy•nu
nid•gol ye•ma•lé Adonái kol - mish•a•lo•té•cha.

Track 17

CONFESSING THE HEBREW SCRIPTURES

Adonai Yireh – יְהֹוָה יִרְאֶה
"THE LORD WILL PROVIDE"

Taste and see how good ADONAI is. Blessed is the one who takes refuge in Him. Fear ADONAI, His kedoshim, For those who fear Him lack nothing.

Psalms 34:9,10

טַעֲמוּ וּרְאוּ כִּי־טוֹב יְהֹוָה אַשְׁרֵי הַגֶּבֶר יֶחֱסֶה־בּוֹ. יְראוּ אֶת־יְהֹוָה קְדֹשָׁיו כִּי אֵין מַחְסוֹר לִירֵאָיו.

Ta•a•mu oor•oo ki - tov Adonái ash•réi ha•gé•ver
ye•che•sé - bo. Yer•oo et - Adonái ke•do•shav ki
eyn mach•sor liy•re•av.

Track 18

CONFESSING THE HEBREW SCRIPTURES

Adonai Yireh – יְהֹוָה יִרְאֶה
"THE LORD WILL PROVIDE"

*Y*oung lions may lack, and go hungry, but those who seek ADONAI want for no good thing.

Psalm 34:11

כְּפִירִים רָשׁוּ וְרָעֵבוּ וְדֹרְשֵׁי יהוה לֹא-יַחְסְרוּ כָל-טוֹב.

Ke•fi•rim ra•shú ve•ra•é•vu ve•dor•shéi Adonái
lo - yach•se•ru chol - tov.

Track 19

CONFESSING THE HEBREW SCRIPTURES

Adonai Yireh – יְהֹוָה יִרְאֶה
"THE LORD WILL PROVIDE"

Cast your burden on ADONAI, and He will sustain you. He will never let the righteous be shaken.

Psalm 55:23

הַשְׁלֵךְ עַל־יְהוָה יְהָבְךָ וְהוּא יְכַלְכְּלֶךָ לֹא־יִתֵּן לְעוֹלָם מוֹט לַצַּדִּיק.

Hash•lech al - Adonái ye•hav•cha ve•hu ye•chal•ke•lé•cha
lo - yi•ten le•o•lam mot la•tza•dik.

CONFESSING THE HEBREW SCRIPTURES

Adonai Yireh – יְהֹוָה יִרְאֶה
"THE LORD WILL PROVIDE"

*Y*ou crown the year with Your goodness. Your wagon tracks drip with abundance.

Psalm 65:12

עָטַרְתָּ שְׁנַת טוֹבָתֶךָ וּמַעְגָּלֶיךָ יִרְעֲפוּן דָּשֶׁן.

Ee·tár·ta sh'nat to·va·té·cha oo·ma·a·ga·lé·cha
yir·a·foon dá·shen.

Track 21

CONFESSING THE HEBREW SCRIPTURES

Adonai Yireh – יְהוָֹה יִרְאֶה

"THE LORD WILL PROVIDE"

For ADONAI *Elohim is a sun and a shield.* ADONAI *gives grace and glory. No good thing will He withhold from those who walk uprightly.*

Psalm 84:12

כִּי שֶׁמֶשׁ וּמָגֵן יְהוָה אֱלֹהִים חֵן וְכָבוֹד יִתֵּן יְהוָה לֹא-יִמְנַע טוֹב לַהֹלְכִים בְּתָמִים.

Ki shé•mesh oo•ma•gen Adonái Elohím chen ve•cha•vod
yi•ten Adonái lo - yim•na tov la•hol•chim be•ta•mim.

Track 22

CONFESSING THE HEBREW SCRIPTURES

Adonai Yireh – יְהֹוָה יִרְאֶה
"THE LORD WILL PROVIDE"

*F*or He will rescue you from the hunter's trap and from the deadly pestilence. He will cover you with His feathers, and under His wings you will find refuge. His faithfulness is body armor and shield.

Psalms 91:3,4

כִּי הוּא יַצִּילְךָ מִפַּח יָקוּשׁ מִדֶּבֶר הַוֹּת. בְּאֶבְרָתוֹ יָסֶךְ לָךְ
וְתַחַת כְּנָפָיו תֶּחְסֶה צִנָּה וְסֹחֵרָה אֲמִתּוֹ.

Ki hoo ya•tzil•cha mi•pach ya•koosh mi•dé•ver ha•vot.
Be•ev•ra•to yá•sech lach ve•tá•chat ke•na•fav tech•sé
tzi•na ve•so•che•rá ami•to.

CONFESSING THE HEBREW SCRIPTURES

Adonai Yireh – יְהֹוָה יִרְאֶה
"THE LORD WILL PROVIDE"

You will not fear the terror by night, nor the arrow that flies by day, nor the plague that stalks in darkness, nor the scourge that lays waste at noon. A thousand may fall at your side, and ten thousand at your right hand, but it will not come near you.

Psalms 91:5-7

לֹא־תִירָא מִפַּחַד לָיְלָה מֵחֵץ יָעוּף יוֹמָם. מִדֶּבֶר בָּאֹפֶל יַהֲלֹךְ מִקֶּטֶב יָשׁוּד צָהֳרָיִם. יִפֹּל מִצִּדְּךָ אֶלֶף וּרְבָבָה מִימִינֶךָ אֵלֶיךָ לֹא יִגָּשׁ.

Lo - ti•ra mi•pá•chad lái•la me•chetz ya•oof yo•mam.
Mi•dé•ver ba•ó•fel yaha•loch mi•ké•tev ya•shood
tzo•ho•rá•yim. Yi•pol mi•tzid•cha é•lef oor•va•va
mi•ye•mi•né•cha e•lé•cha lo yi•gash.

Track 24

CONFESSING THE HEBREW SCRIPTURES

Adonai Yireh – יְהֹוָה יִרְאֶה
"THE LORD WILL PROVIDE"

He causes grass to spring up for the cattle, and vegetation for man to cultivate, to bring forth bread out of the earth, wine that makes man's heart glad, oil to make his face shine, and bread that sustains man's heart.

Psalms 104:14,15

מַצְמִיחַ חָצִיר לַבְּהֵמָה וְעֵשֶׂב לַעֲבֹדַת הָאָדָם לְהוֹצִיא
לֶחֶם מִן-הָאָרֶץ. וְיַיִן יְשַׂמַּח לְבַב-אֱנוֹשׁ לְהַצְהִיל פָּנִים
מִשָּׁמֶן וְלֶחֶם לְבַב-אֱנוֹשׁ יִסְעָד.

Matz·mí·ach cha·tzir la·be·he·ma ve·é·sev la·avo·dat
ha·adám le·ho·tzi lé·chem min - ha·á·retz. Ve·yá·yin
ye·sa·mach le·vav - enosh le·hatz·hil pa·nim
mi·shá·men ve·lé·chem le·vav - enosh yis·ad.

CONFESSING THE HEBREW SCRIPTURES

Adonai Yireh – יְהֹוָה יִרְאֶה

"THE LORD WILL PROVIDE"

He made His wonders memorable. ADONAI is gracious and full of compassion. He gives food to those who fear Him. He remembers His covenant forever.

Psalms 111:4,5

זֵכֶר עָשָׂה לְנִפְלְאוֹתָיו חַנּוּן וְרַחוּם יְהוָה. טֶרֶף נָתַן לִירֵאָיו יִזְכֹּר לְעוֹלָם בְּרִיתוֹ.

Zé·cher asa le·nif·le·o·tav cha·noon ve·ra·choom Adonái.
Té·ref na·tan li·re·av yiz·kor le·o·lam be·ri·to.

Track 26

CONFESSING THE HEBREW SCRIPTURES

Adonai Yireh – יְהוָֹה יִרְאֶה
"THE LORD WILL PROVIDE"

For through me your days will be many and years will be added to your life.

Proverbs 9:11

כִּי-בִי יִרְבּוּ יָמֶיךָ וְיוֹסִיפוּ לְךָ שְׁנוֹת חַיִּים.

Ki - vi yir•bu ya•mé•cha ve•yo•sí•fu le•chá sh'not cha•yím.

CONFESSING THE HEBREW SCRIPTURES

Adonai Yireh – יְהֹוָה יִרְאֶה
"THE LORD WILL PROVIDE"

The reward of humility and fear of ADONAI is riches, honor and life.

Proverbs 22:4

עֵקֶב עֲנָוָה יִרְאַת יְהֹוָה עֹשֶׁר וְכָבוֹד וְחַיִּים.

Ékev ana•va yir•at Adonái ó•sher ve•cha•vod ve•cha•yím.

CONFESSING THE HEBREW SCRIPTURES

Adonai Yireh – יְהֹוָה יִרְאֶה
"THE LORD WILL PROVIDE"

Even to your old age I will be the same, until you are gray I will carry you. I have done it; I will bear you; I will carry you; I will deliver you.

Isaiah 46:4

וְעַד-זִקְנָה אֲנִי הוּא וְעַד-שֵׂיבָה אֲנִי אֶסְבֹּל אֲנִי עָשִׂיתִי
וַאֲנִי אֶשָּׂא וַאֲנִי אֶסְבֹּל וַאֲמַלֵּט.

Ve•ad - zik•na Ani hoo ve•ad - sei•va Ani es•bol
Ani así•ti va•Ani esa va•Ani es•bol va•ama•let.

Track 29

CONFESSING THE HEBREW SCRIPTURES

Adonai Yireh – יְהוָה יִרְאֶה
"THE LORD WILL PROVIDE"

Then ADONAI will guide you continually, satisfy your soul in drought and strengthen your bones. You will be like a watered garden, like a spring of water whose waters never fail.

Isaiah 58:11

וְנָחֲךָ יְהוָה תָּמִיד וְהִשְׂבִּיעַ בְּצַחְצָחוֹת נַפְשֶׁךָ וְעַצְמֹתֶיךָ יַחֲלִיץ
וְהָיִיתָ כְּגַן רָוֶה וּכְמוֹצָא מַיִם אֲשֶׁר לֹא-יְכַזְּבוּ מֵימָיו.

Ve•na•cha•cha Adonái ta•mid ve•his•bía be•tzach•tza•chot
naf•shé•cha ve•atz•mo•té•cha ya•cha•litz ve•ha•yí•ta ke•gan
ra•vé oo•che•mo•tza má•yim ashér lo - ye•chaz•vu mei•mav.

Track 30

CONFESSING THE HEBREW SCRIPTURES

Adonai Yireh – יְהֹוָה יִרְאֶה
"THE LORD WILL PROVIDE"

*B*lessed is the one who trusts in ADONAI, whose confidence is in ADONAI. For he will be like a tree planted by the waters, spreading out its roots by a stream. It has no fear when heat comes, but its leaves will be green. It does not worry in a year of drought, nor depart from yielding fruit.

Jeremiah 17:7,8

בָּרוּךְ הַגֶּבֶר אֲשֶׁר יִבְטַח בַּיהוָה וְהָיָה יְהוָה מִבְטַחוֹ. וְהָיָה
כְּעֵץ שָׁתוּל עַל-מַיִם וְעַל-יוּבַל יְשַׁלַּח שָׁרָשָׁיו וְלֹא
(יְרָא) [יִרְאֶה] כִּי-יָבֹא חֹם וְהָיָה עָלֵהוּ רַעֲנָן וּבִשְׁנַת בַּצֹּרֶת
לֹא יִדְאָג וְלֹא יָמִישׁ מֵעֲשׂוֹת פֶּרִי.

Ba•rúch ha•gé•ver ashér yiv•tach ba•Adonái ve•ha•ya
Adonái miv•ta•cho. Ve•ha•ya ke•etz sha•tool al - má•yim
ve•al - yu•val ye•sha•lách sho•ra•shav ve•lo (yi•re) [yir•eh]
ki - ya•vo chom ve•ha•ya alé•hu ra•a•nan oo•vish•nat
ba•tzó•ret lo yid•ag ve•lo ya•mish me•a•sot péri.

CONFESSING THE HEBREW SCRIPTURES

Adonai Yireh – יְהוָֹה יִרְאֶה
"THE LORD WILL PROVIDE"

Ask ADONAI for rain in spring! ADONAI makes the storm clouds and will give rain showers and plants of the field to everyone.

Zechariah 10:1

שַׁאֲלוּ מֵיְהוָה מָטָר בְּעֵת מַלְקוֹשׁ יְהוָה עֹשֶׂה חֲזִיזִים
וּמְטַר-גֶּשֶׁם יִתֵּן לָהֶם לְאִישׁ עֵשֶׂב בַּשָּׂדֶה.

Sha•a•lu me•Adonái ma•tar be•et mal•kosh Adonái
o•sé cha•zi•zim oo•me•tar - gé•shem yi•ten la•hém
le•eesh é•sev ba•sa•dé.

Confessing the Hebrew Scriptures

Adonai Yireh – יְרָאֶה יְהֹוָה
"THE LORD WILL PROVIDE"

Look at the birds of the air. They do not sow or reap or gather into barns; yet your Father in heaven feeds them. Are you not of more value than they?

Matthew 6:26

הַבִּיטוּ אֶל-עוֹף הַשָּׁמַיִם לֹא יִזְרְעוּ לֹא יִקְצְרוּ וְלֹא יַאַסְפוּ
לִמְגוּרוֹת וַאֲבִיכֶם בַּשָּׁמַיִם מְכַלְכֵּל אֹתָם וְאַתֶּם הֲלֹא נַעֲלֵיתֶם
יֶתֶר הַרְבֵּה עֲלֵיהֶם.

Ha•bí•tu el - of ha•sha•má•yim lo yiz•re•oo lo yik•tze•ru
ve•lo ya•as•fu lim•gu•rot va•Avi•chem ba•sha•má•yim
me•chal•kel o•tam ve•a•tem ha•lo na•a•léy•tem yé•ter
har•be aley•hem.

CONFESSING THE HEBREW SCRIPTURES
Adonai Yireh – יְהוָה יִרְאֶה
"THE LORD WILL PROVIDE"

But seek first the kingdom of God and His righteousness, and all these things shall be added to you.

Matthew 6:33

אַךְ בַּקְשׁוּ רִאשֹׁנָה מַלְכוּת אֱלֹהִים וְצִדְקָתוֹ וְכָל-הַחֲפָצִים הָהֵם יִנָּתְנוּ לָכֶם מַתָּנוֹת נוֹסָפוֹת.

Ach bak•shu ri•sho•na mal•choot Elohim ve•tzid•ka•to ve•chol - ha•cha•fa•tzim ha•hem yi•nat•nu la•chem ma•ta•not no•sa•fot.

CONFESSING THE HEBREW SCRIPTURES

Adonai Yireh – יְהוָה יִרְאֶה
"THE LORD WILL PROVIDE"

If you then, being evil, know how to give good gifts to your children, how much more will your Father in heaven give good things to those who ask Him!

Matthew 7:11

וְאַף כִּי רָעִים אַתֶּם תֵּדְעוּן לָתֵת מַתָּנוֹת טֹבוֹת לִבְנֵיכֶם אַף כִּי־אֲבִיכֶם שֶׁבַּשָּׁמַיִם יִתֶּן־טוֹב לְדֹרְשָׁיו.

Ve•af ki ra•eem atem ted•oon la•tet
ma•ta•not to•vot liv•ney•chem af ki - Avi•chem
she•ba•sha•má•yim yi•ten - tov le•dor•shav.

Track 35

CONFESSING THE HEBREW SCRIPTURES

Adonai Yireh – יְהֹוָה יִרְאֶה
"THE LORD WILL PROVIDE"

And whatever you ask in prayer, trusting, you shall receive.

Matthew 21:22

וְכָל-דָּבָר אֲשֶׁר תִּשְׁאֲלוּ בִתְפִלָּה אִם רַק בֶּאֱמוּנָה
שְׁאֶלְתֶּם יִתַּן לָכֶם.

Ve•chol - da•var asher tish•a•lu vit•fi•la eem rak
be•e•mu•na sh•el•tem yoo•tan la•chem.

CONFESSING THE HEBREW SCRIPTURES

Adonai Yireh – יְהֹוָה יִרְאֶה
"THE LORD WILL PROVIDE"

Give, and it will be given to you—a good measure, pressed down, shaken together, overflowing, will be given into your lap. For whatever measure you measure out will be measured back to you.

Luke 6:38

תְּנוּ וְיִנָּתֵן לָכֶם מִדָּה מְלֵאָה עַל־כָּל־גְּדוֹתֶיהָ יָשִׁיבוּ אֶל־חֵיקְכֶם
אֲשֶׁר יָעִיקוּ תַּחְתֶּיהָ וַאֲשֶׁר יָנִיעוּ אֹתָהּ כִּי בְּסַאסְאָה אֲשֶׁר
תָּמֹדּוּ בָּהּ יִמַּד לָכֶם.

Te•nu ve•yi•na•ten la•chem mi•da me•le•ah
al - kol - ge•do•té•ha ya•shí•vu el - cheyk•chem asher
ya•ée•ku tach•té•ha va•a•sher ya•ní•oo o•ta ki
ve•sa•se•ah asher ta•mó•du ba yim•ad la•chem.

CONFESSING THE HEBREW SCRIPTURES

Adonai Yireh – יְהֹוָה יִרְאֶה

"THE LORD WILL PROVIDE"

...So I say to you, do not worry about life, what you will eat; nor about the body, what you will wear. But if God so clothes the grass in the field—which is here today and thrown into the furnace tomorrow—then how much more will He clothe you, O you of little faith?

Luke: 12:22,28

...עַל-כֵּן אֲנִי אֹמֵר לָכֶם לֹא תָחוּשׁוּ לְנַפְשְׁכֶם לֵאמֹר מַה-נֹּאכֵל
אוֹ לִבְשַׂרְכֶם מַה-נִּלְבָּשׁ. וְאִם-כָּכָה יַעֲטֶה אֱלֹהִים אֶת-עֵשֶׂב
הַשָּׂדֶה אֲשֶׁר יָצִיץ הַיּוֹם וּלְמָחֳרָתוֹ יֻתַּן בַּתַּנּוּר אַף כִּי-אֶתְכֶם
קְטַנֵּי אֱמָנָה.

...al - ken ani o•mer la•chem lo ta•chú•shu le•naf•she•chem
le•mor ma - no•chel o liv•sar•chem ma - nil•bash.
Ve•eem - ká•cha ya•a•te Elohim et - e•sev ha•sa•de a•sher
ya•tzitz ha•yom ool•mo•cho•ra•to yoo•tan ba•ta•noor af
ki - et•chem ke•ta•ney e•mu•na.

CONFESSING THE HEBREW SCRIPTURES

Adonai Yireh – יְהֹוָה יִרְאֶה
"THE LORD WILL PROVIDE"

You did not choose Me, but I chose you. I selected you so that you would go and produce fruit, and your fruit would remain. Then the Father will give you whatever you ask in My name."

John 15:16

לֹא אַתֶּם בְּחַרְתֶּם בִּי רַק-אֲנִי בָחַרְתִּי בָּכֶם וַאֲנִי מִנִּיתִי אֶתְכֶם
לָלֶכֶת וְלַעֲשׂוֹת פְּרִי וּפֶרְיְכֶם יַעֲמֹד לָעַד וְכָל-דָּבָר אֲשֶׁר תִּשְׁאֲלוּ
מֵאֵת הָאָב בִּשְׁמִי אֹתוֹ יִתֵּן לָכֶם.

Lo a•tem be•char•tem bi rak - ani ba•chár•ti ba•chem
va•a•ni mi•ní•ti et•chem la•lé•chet ve•la•a•sot pé•ri
oo•fer•ye•chem ya•a•mod la•ad ve•chol - da•var asher
tish•a•lu me•et ha•Av bish•mi o•to yi•ten la•chem.

Track 39

CONFESSING THE HEBREW SCRIPTURES

Adonai Yireh – יְהֹוָה יִרְאֶה
"THE LORD WILL PROVIDE"

...Amen, amen I tell you, whatever you ask the Father in My name, He will give you.

John 16:23

‏...אָמֵן אָמֵן אֲנִי אֹמֵר לָכֶם אִם תְּבַקְשׁוּ
דָבָר מֵאֵת הָאָב יִתֵּן לָכֶם בִּשְׁמִי.

...Amen amen ani o•mer la•chem eem te•vak•shu
da•var me•et ha•Av yi•ten la•chem bish•mi.

Track 40

CONFESSING THE HEBREW SCRIPTURES

Adonai Yireh – יְהֹוָה יִרְאֶה
"THE LORD WILL PROVIDE"

He who did not spare His own Son but gave Him up for us all, how shall He not also with Him freely give us all things?

Romans 8:32

הֵן הוּא לֹא חָמַל עַל בֶּן-סְגֻלָּתוֹ כִּי אִם-הִסְגִּירוֹ בְּעַד כֻּלָּנוּ
הֲכִי עִמּוֹ לֹא יִתֶּן-לָנוּ כָּל-מִשְׁאֲלוֹתֵינוּ כְּרֹב חַסְדּוֹ.

Hen hoo lo cha•mal al ben - se•goo•la•to ki
eem - his•gi•ro be•ad ku•lá•nu ha•chi ee•mo lo
yi•ten - lá•nu kol - mish•a•lo•téy•nu ke•rov chas•do.

Track 41

Confessing the Hebrew Scriptures

Adonai Yireh – יְהֹוָה יִרְאֶה
"THE LORD WILL PROVIDE"

And God is able to bless you abundantly, so that in all things at all times, having all that you need, you will abound in every good work.

2 Corinthians 9:8

וְיַד אֱלֹהִים מַשֶּׂגֶת לִשְׁפֹּת לָכֶם כָּל-חָסֶד לְמַלֵּא דֵי מַחְסֹרְכֶם כָּל-הַיָּמִים וְלָתֵת לָכֶם חַיִל לַעֲשׂוֹת כָּל-טוֹב.

Ve•yad Elohim ma•sé•get lish•pot la•chem kol - chá•sed
le•ma•le dey mach•sor•chem kol - ha•ya•mim ve•la•tet
la•chem chá•yil la•a•sot kol - tov.

CONFESSING THE HEBREW SCRIPTURES

Adonai Yireh – יְהֹוָה יִרְאֶה
"THE LORD WILL PROVIDE"

Now he who supplies seed to the sower and bread for food will also supply and increase your store of seed and will enlarge the harvest of your righteousness. You will be enriched in every way so that you can be generous on every occasion, and through us your generosity will result in thanksgiving to God.

2 Corinthians 9:10,11

וְהַנֹּתֵן זֶרַע לַזֹּרֵעַ וְלֶחֶם לָאֹכֵל כֹּה יִתֵּן וְכֹה יוֹסִף לָכֶם
אֶת-זַרְעֲכֶם וְאֶת-פְּרִי צִדְקַתְכֶם יַרְבֶּה. כִּי תִתְבָּרְכוּ בַּכֹּל
בְּכָל-מַעֲשֵׂה נְדִיבוֹת לְהַשְׁמִיעַ תְּהִלַּת אֱלֹהִים עַל-יָדֵינוּ.

Ve•ha•no•ten zé•ra la•zo•réa ve•lé•chem la•o•chél ko
yi•ten ve•cho yo•sif la•chem et - zar•a•chem ve•et - p'ri
tzid•kat•chem yar•be. Ki tit•bará•chu va•kol
be•chol - ma•a•se ne•di•vot le•hash•mí•a te•hi•lat
Elohim al - ya•déy•nu.

Track 43

CONFESSING THE HEBREW SCRIPTURES

Adonai Yireh – יְהֹוָה יִרְאֶה
"THE LORD WILL PROVIDE"

Now to Him who is able to do far beyond all that we ask or imagine, by means of His power that works in us

Ephesians 3:20

וְהוּא אֲשֶׁר יָדָיו רַב לוֹ לְעוֹרֵר בַּכֹּחַ לִבֵּנוּ וְלַעֲשׂוֹת לָנוּ
יֶתֶר עַל־כָּל־מִשְׁאֲלוֹתֵינוּ וּמַחְשְׁבוֹתֵינוּ:

Ve•hoo a•sher ya•dav rav lo le•o•rer ba•kó•ach
li•bé•nu ve•la•a•sot lá•nu yé•ter
al - kol - mish•a•lo•téy•nu oo•mach•she•vo•téy•nu.

CONFESSING THE HEBREW SCRIPTURES

Adonai Yireh – יְהֹוָה יִרְאֶה
"THE LORD WILL PROVIDE"

My God will fulfill every need of yours according to the riches of His glory in Messiah Yeshua.

Philippians 4:19

וֵאלֹהַי יְמַלֵּא כָל-מַחְסֹרְכֶם בְּעָשְׁרוֹ וּבִכְבוֹדוֹ בְּיֵשׁוּעַ הַמָּשִׁיחַ.

VE•lohai ye•ma•le chol - mach•sor•chem be•osh•ro
oo•vich•vodo be•Yeshua ha•Ma•shi•ach.

Track 45

CONFESSING THE HEBREW SCRIPTURES

Adonai Yireh – יְהוָֹה יִרְאֶה
"THE LORD WILL PROVIDE"

Direct those who are rich in this present age not to be proud or to fix their hope on the uncertainty of riches, but rather on God—who richly provides us with everything to enjoy.

I Timothy 6:17

צַו עַל-עֲשִׁירֵי הָעוֹלָם הַזֶּה לְבִלְתִּי יָרוּם לְבָבָם
וְלֹא-יִבְטְחוּ בְעֹשֶׁר אֲשֶׁר כְּנָפַיִם לוֹ כִּי אִם-בֵּאלֹהִים
הַנֹּתֵן לָנוּ דַי וְהוֹתֵר לִשְׂבֹּעַ.

Tzav al - ashi•rey ha•o•lam ha•ze le•vil•ti ya•room
le•va•vam ve•lo - yiv•te•choo va•ó•sher asher
ke•na•fá•yim lo ki eem - be•Elohim ha•no•ten lá•nu
dai ve•ho•ter lis•bó•a.